Contents

KU-092-285

When kittens are born
At first, newborn
kittens cannot see
or hear. When they
are three months old,
they can see and hear
very well.

Let's Read About Pets

Kittens

JoAnn Early Macken

Reading consultant: Susan Nations

FRANKLIN WATTS

Schools Library and Information Services

S00000672414

DUBLEY PUBLIC LIBRARIES

L 48001

672414 | SCH

J 636.8

First UK hardback edition 2004
First UK paperback edition 2005

Franklin Watts
96 Leonard Street
London EC2A 4XD

Franklin Watts Australia
45-51 Huntley Street
Alexandria
NSW 2015

Copyright © 2004 by Weekly Reader Early Learning Library

ISBN 0 7496 5759 6 (hardback)
ISBN 0 7496 5826 6 (paperback)

Published in association with Weekly Reader Early Learning Library, Milwaukee.

All rights reserved. No part of this book may be reproduced, stored in a retrieval system,
or transmitted in any form or by any means, electronic, mechanical, photocopying, recording
or otherwise, without the prior written permission of the copyright holder.

Printed in Hong Kong, China

Eating and drinking

A newborn kitten drinks its mother's milk. A few weeks later, it can eat solid food. Kittens also need fresh water.

A kitten's eyes

All kittens have blue eyes when they are born. A kitten's eyes may change colour when it gets older.

A kitten's fur

A kitten's fur may be long or short. It can be white, black, orange, grey or a mixture of colours. It sometimes has stripes or spots.

Keeping clean

Kittens lick their fur to keep it clean. You can brush your kitten's fur to keep it free from knots and tangles.

Using its tail

A kitten's tail is part of its backbone. A kitten uses its tail to balance.

Making sounds

A kitten may mew or miaow when it sees you. When you hold a kitten it sometimes purrs. An angry kitten might growl, hiss or spit.

Playtime!

A kitten starts to play when it is about four weeks old. It may pounce on a toy or chase a ball.

Time to rest

After all that work, a kitten needs to rest! All kittens need a lot of sleep.

New words

pounce — to jump on something and grab it

purr — a low rumbling sound made by a happy cat

solid food — dried food or food from a tin

tangles — knots

How to find out more

Here are some useful websites about kittens:

http://aolsvc.petplace.aol.com
Click on "Cats" in Pet Centers, then click on Featured
Articles "Just for Kids" to find where your cat should sleep,
your kitten's first six weeks, and other facts

www.pdsa.org.uk
Click on "You and your pet" and then click on "Kittens
and cats" to find useful advice

www.abc.net.au/creaturefeatures/facts/kittens.htm
Information on everything from making your kitten feel at
home to protecting furniture from cat scratches

> **Note** We strongly advise that Internet access is
> supervised by a responsible adult.

Index

Notes for teachers and parents

This book is specially designed to support the young reader in the reading process. The familiar topic is appealing to young children and invites them to read — and re-read — the book again and again. The full-colour photographs and enhanced text help the child during the reading process. After children develop fluency with the text and content, the book can be read independently.